Six-Word Lessons to Rise and Shine— A Journey Within

100 Lessons for Healing, Hope and Wholeness

Cheri L. Jackson

Published by Pacelli Publishing
Bellevue, Washington

Six-Word Lessons to Rise and Shine—A Journey Within

All rights reserved. No part of this book may be reproduced or transmitted in any form or by any means, electronic or mechanical including photocopying, recording or by any information storage or retrieval system, without the written permission of the publisher, except where permitted by law.

Limit of Liability: While the author and the publisher have used their best efforts in preparing this book, they make no representation or warranties with respect to the accuracy or completeness of the content of this book. The advice and strategies contained herein may not be suitable for your situation. Consult with a professional when appropriate.

Cover and interior designed by Pacelli Publishing
Cover photo by Jimsngjung via Pixabay.com

Copyright © 2025 by Cheri L. Jackson

Published by Pacelli Publishing
9905 Lake Washington Blvd. NE, #D-103
Bellevue, Washington 98004
PacelliPublishing.com

ISBN 10: 1-967256-01-2
ISBN-13: 978-1-967256-01-3

Dedication

To my Heavenly Father, who never stopped pursuing me: Your love has always been there, waiting for me to fully surrender. Thank you for guiding me home.

To my Lord Jesus, my Savior and Redeemer: You pulled me from the darkness, healed my heart, and showed me who I truly am. Because of You, I walk in freedom.

To Holy Spirit, my Teacher, Counselor, and Guide: Your whispers have shaped my path, teaching me to trust, listen, and follow without fear.

To my family and those who have walked alongside me: Thank you for loving me through every season.

And to you, the reader: I see you. I know the longing in your heart, the questions, the desire for something more. May this book be a light on your path, a reminder that you are never alone. You were made for more. It's time to rise and shine.

Contents

Introduction 7

In the Beginning: Awakening the Soul 9

Stepping into Truth: Embracing Joy,
 Facing Reality 21

Surrender: Release, Receive, Transcend,
 Transforming Life 31

Cultivate Spiritual Bond:
 Deepening Connection's Roots 41

Mindset Shift: Choosing Faith Over Fear 53

Answer the Call; Embrace Your Purpose 65

Release Doubt and Judgement:
 Elevate Spirit 77

Embrace What Is: Find Serenity Within 89

Recognize Our Teachers—Divine Guidance's
 Whispers 101

See It, Believe It, Become It 113

Introduction

There comes a moment when life invites us to step beyond who we've been and into who we were always meant to be.

This book is about that journey.

I searched for love, healing, and purpose in all the wrong places—believing that if I just worked harder, achieved more, or found the right relationship, I would finally feel whole. But no matter what I did, the emptiness remained. It wasn't until I surrendered my life to Jesus Christ as my Lord and Savior, received and embraced Holy Spirit, sat under His tutelage, and took the time to really know my Heavenly Father that everything changed.

This book isn't just another book—it's an invitation to transformation. Through personal stories, powerful insights, and Holy Spirit revelations, I share the lessons that shaped me, the struggles that refined me, and the faith that restored me.

But this isn't just my story—it's yours too.

As you turn these pages, you may see parts of yourself reflected in my journey. You may recognize struggles you've faced, questions you've wrestled with, and longings you've carried. My prayer is that through these words, you will be encouraged, strengthened, and awakened to the truth of who you are in Christ.

You didn't pick up this book by accident. Something inside you is stirring—a desire for more, a longing for healing, a call to rise into the person you were always meant to be. My prayer is that as you walk through these pages, you will discover the truth of who you already are in Christ and step boldly into the life God created for you.

You are not alone. You are not forgotten. You are not too far gone.

This is your time to rise. This is your time to shine.

In the Beginning: Awakening the Soul

Joy's essence: embracing childhood's pure radiance

I came into this world full of joy—laughing, playing, and freely expressing myself. But life has a way of dimming that light. My parents' constant fighting, drinking, and eventual divorce forced me into survival mode. Still, joy wasn't gone; it was just buried. Think back—when was the last time you felt pure, unfiltered happiness? That feeling isn't lost; it's still part of you, waiting to shine again.

Life's challenges: building inner strength within

My parents did their best, but they struggled to provide the love and security I needed. I longed for acceptance, but their own battles kept them distant. I had to be strong, even when I felt unseen. Through every hardship, I learned to rely on myself. Those challenges didn't just make me stronger—they made me independent. How have your struggles shaped your inner strength?

Independence quest: stepping boldly into adulthood

At 16, leaving home didn't feel like a choice—it felt like survival. I believed I could do a better job of keeping myself safe, so I left, convinced I was taking control of my future. But independence didn't bring the security I imagined. I worked, went to school, and searched for meaning. Freedom wasn't just about escaping; it was about figuring out who I was. Have you ever mistaken survival for independence?

Love's illusion: searching for worth externally

I spent years searching for love in all the wrong places, like relationships, achievements, food, and substances—anything to numb the emptiness inside. I craved validation, believing if I could just be enough, I'd finally feel complete. But nothing truly filled me. The harder I searched, the more lost I became. Where have you sought love outside yourself?

Reflecting inward: discovering self-worth within

I spent a lifetime chasing love, believing someone else could make me feel whole. Relationship after relationship, I clung to hope, only to end up empty. Then one day, I looked in the mirror and asked myself, Who am I, really? That question cracked something open. Love isn't something we chase—it's something we build within. What parts of you still long to be seen and loved by you?

Crossroads encounter: choosing survival or transformation

My life wasn't sustainable. I wanted more, but didn't know how to break free. I believed a stable career in community corrections would be my fresh start, but they valued compliance over transformation. I had to choose: stay in a path that felt safe or step into the unknown. Have you ever realized that real change requires leaving something behind?

Turning point: awakening to life's purpose

Even when I was lost, something inside me whispered that I was meant to help others. I didn't know how or why, but the desire was there. Over time, I started listening—to myself, to others, to God. The message was clear: I had a calling. And it kept whispering, Write. Teach. Lead. Purpose isn't a job title, it's what's been calling you all along. What is life trying to tell you right now?

Identity reclaimed: releasing illusions, embracing truth

I spent years believing success, approval, and achievements would finally make me feel worthy. I worked hard, excelled, and kept pushing—but nothing ever felt like enough. No title, no accomplishment could fill the void inside me. Then, I realized my worth had never been something to earn—it had always been there. Where in your life have you been chasing validation instead of embracing your true worth?

Breaking cycles: overcoming addiction, finding wholeness

I saw the patterns—the self-sabotage, the unhealthy choices, the same cycles playing on repeat. It took work, deep work, to break free, such as therapy, faith, and hard conversations with myself. But I did it. And you can too. Healing isn't a single breakthrough; it's a daily choice to rewrite the story. What pattern in your life needs to end so you can create something new?

10

New direction beckons. Spiritual awakening initiated.

I had spent my life searching, striving, and running in circles, trying to fill the emptiness inside. Nothing ever lasted. Something had to change. One night, exhausted and broken, I fell to my knees and surrendered my life to Jesus. I welcomed Him into my heart, knowing only He could fill the void. My soul was awakening. What would happen if you fully surrendered to Jesus?

Stepping into Truth: Embracing Joy, Facing Reality

Seeking truth: a deeper call begins.

After surrendering my life to Jesus, something inside me shifted. I felt lighter, freer—like a weight had lifted. I started humming some of my favorite tunes, changing the lyrics and singing them to Jesus. I couldn't stop thinking about Him, couldn't stop talking to Him. I finally knew what it meant to be in love with Jesus. How is Jesus drawing you closer to Him?

12

Sharing my truth: an unexpected cost

Falling in love with Jesus was effortless and I eagerly shared my transformation, expecting others to celebrate with me. But not everyone was ready. Friends distanced themselves, relationships shifted, and I mourned the unexpected losses. God reminded me that only He knows each heart's readiness. My job wasn't to convince—it was to trust Him. Who in your life have you tried to reach, only to find they weren't ready?

Releasing control: trusting God's timing

Losing relationships because of my faith hurt, but I realized I couldn't make people see what they weren't ready for. I wanted everyone to experience what I had, but faith can't be forced. God moves in His timing, not mine. Instead of mourning what I lost, I sought out new, like-minded relationships. Where in your life do you need to release control and trust God's timing?

Seeking more: embracing a retreat opportunity

A longing stirred in me—I needed more. Joy wasn't enough; I craved deeper understanding and connection. Then, my church announced a weeklong retreat with evangelists from South Africa. It felt like an opportunity, a divine setup. Stepping into that space, I felt a new sense of belonging. Then, for the first time, I heard Holy Spirit clearly. My journey was unfolding. When have you longed for something more?

Seeking God's truth beyond the experience

During the retreat, I stepped forward at an altar call, expecting an encounter with God. Around me, people were slain in the Spirit, falling as they encountered Him. But I remained standing, tears streaming. The "catchers" expected me to fall, but Holy Spirit was teaching me: Seek Me, not the experience. Faith is connection, not appearance. When have you felt pressured to conform rather than be real in your faith?

16

Seeking more: deceived by the counterfeit

Still longing for more, I convinced myself I was seeking God—not just an experience. A church member invited me to visit his mother's church, where people were "drunk in the Spirit." Curious and hungry, I went. But something felt off. The energy was strong but not holy. I didn't realize it, but I had stepped into deception. Have you ever pursued something that seemed good but later proved harmful?

Discernment matters: recognizing the enemy's counterfeit

That same night, I had terrifying dreams—demons trying to take me. I cried out to Jesus and woke up shaken. I had sought an experience and found deception instead. My spiritual mentor confirmed my worst fear: the church was Satanic. I finally understood—seek God, not just the experience. True faith requires discernment. When have you ignored red flags, only to later realize the danger?

Rooted in truth: the journey continues.

I had learned a hard but vital lesson—true faith isn't about chasing emotions; it's about surrendering to God's truth. No longer swayed by spiritual highs, I sought a deeper, lasting connection with Him. Discernment became essential—would I trust what God was showing me, even when it challenged me? Truth wasn't a destination—it was a lifelong pursuit. Where is God calling you to surrender to His truth?

Surrender: Release, Receive, Transcend, Transforming Life

Surrender happens daily, not just once.

Surrender wasn't a one-time event—it was a daily choice. I thought giving my life to Jesus meant I had fully surrendered, but I soon realized I was still holding on to control, fear, and self-reliance. Each day, God invited me to release, trust, and follow Him completely. The question wasn't, "Have I surrendered?" but "Am I surrendering right now?" What are you still holding onto?

20

Release control and fear to surrender.

Even after surrendering, I fought to hold on. What if I let go and everything fell apart? Fear told me I needed control, but surrender invited me into peace, not chaos. The more I released, the more I felt truly free—more in control than I had ever been. True control wasn't in gripping tightly but in trusting God completely. What are you still afraid to release?

The Holy Spirit's gentle, personal whisper

Letting go of control felt freeing, but something deeper was happening. I wasn't just talking to God—I was hearing Him. Then Holy Spirit whispered, "It's been Me all along." I had believed Jesus spoke through my thoughts, but now I knew—the voice guiding me had always been Him. Never forceful, always present, leading me forward. How have you sensed the Holy Spirit's voice in your life?

Trusting His voice begins with surrender.

I told Holy Spirit, "When I hear Your voice, I will obey." But I had to learn to discern His voice first. That meant surrendering my assumptions, slowing down, and intentionally acknowledging Him throughout the day. The more I listened, the clearer His voice became. Surrender wasn't just about letting go—it was about choosing to trust and follow. How would your life change if you truly listened?

Facing the past: healing through truth

God began bringing to mind those I had hurt. Instead of drowning in shame, I felt His invitation to heal. Confronting my past was painful, but healing required truth. Avoidance kept me bound; honesty set me free. Before I could make amends, I had to face the wounds within. What past hurts or mistakes is God prompting you to confront with grace and courage?

24

Repent, forgive, obey: healing will follow

Healing wasn't complete without action. Surrender meant letting go of pride and following God's way. Holy Spirit led me to repent, forgive, and make amends. Avoiding it kept me bound, but obedience set me free. Repentance broke chains, forgiveness healed wounds, and making amends restored what was broken. I didn't have to earn grace—just walk in it. What step of obedience is God calling you to take right now?

Trusting God in joy and trials

Letting go didn't remove struggles—it changed how I faced them. I used to fight for control, believing peace came from certainty. But Holy Spirit showed me true peace isn't found in perfect circumstances—it's found in trust. Joy deepened, trials felt lighter, and faith replaced fear. God was with me in every season. How would your trials change if you fully trusted Him?

Making amends: the power of repentance

Repentance wasn't just saying I was sorry—it was surrendering to God's truth. Making amends required humility, courage, and obedience. I had to trust the outcome to God, even if others didn't receive it well. Surrender meant obedience, even when it was hard. Every step brought freedom. Healing wasn't just for me but those I had hurt too. What act of repentance is God calling you to take today?

Living truth: embracing joy and trials

Living in truth meant trusting God in both joy and trials. Faith didn't erase hardship—it transformed how I walked through it. Surrendering to God's plan gave me peace, even when life felt uncertain. Trials refined my faith, and joy deepened my trust. What would shift in your heart if you fully embraced both joy and trials as part of God's plan?

Cultivate Spiritual Bond: Deepening Connection's Roots

Choosing trust begins the journey forward.

The deeper my relationship with Holy Spirit grew, the more I realized trust wasn't just about surrender—it was about letting go, over and over again. I had spent my life believing I had to hold everything together, but Holy Spirit was teaching me something different. Letting go felt scary, but He kept proving Himself faithful. Where in your life do you need to stop striving and trust Him more?

29

Let Holy Spirit direct your path.

The car wash sign read: "Put the car in neutral, take your foot off the pedals, and hands off the wheel." As I read it, I felt Holy Spirit whisper, 'That's what I want you to do—let Me guide you.' I had spent my life trying to steer my own way, but now I was ready. Trust meant releasing control and allowing Him to lead. Are you ready too?

Learning to trust God your Father

I embraced Jesus and Holy Spirit easily, but I wanted no part of my Heavenly Father. I saw Him as a mean old man in the sky, letting me down when I needed Him most. Deep down, I knew my resistance wasn't just about Him—it was about wounds I hadn't fully faced. Little by little, Holy Spirit nudged me closer. Trust was growing. What past wounds keep you distant?

Gratitude connects you with God's heart.

One winter, my neighbor used his snow blower to clear my driveway. I thanked him but never thought to thank God. Then Holy Spirit whispered, "Oh, so your neighbor did it?" That humbled me—I didn't acknowledge God as my provider. To drive the lesson home, the next snowfall was heavier, and I shoveled alone. Gratitude shifts perspective. Where is God inviting you to recognize His provision today?

Seeking God first transformed my life.

Beginning my day in prayer reshaped my relationship with God. It wasn't just a habit; it was trust in action. Father never pressured me—He waited. As I sought Him, I asked to see myself and others through His eyes. One day, I looked in the mirror and said, "Cheri, I love you." This time, I meant it. How can you start your day by surrendering to His love?

Obedience strengthens trust in God's plan.

One day, Holy Spirit urged me to pray for someone who had hurt me. Everything in me resisted. But I obeyed, and something shifted. As I prayed, my heart softened, releasing pain I hadn't realized I was holding. Healing began in unexpected ways. Obedience isn't about obligation—it's about trusting God's plan, even when it's hard. What act of obedience is God calling you into today?

Seeing myself through my Father's eyes

Love felt conditional—something I had to work for. I measured my worth by what I did, not who I was. But as I prayed for those who hurt me, my heart shifted. I saw myself through Father's eyes—fully loved, no longer striving. And when I saw myself differently, I saw others differently too. How can you ask your Father to show you how He sees you today?

35

Forgiveness frees your heart to heal.

Forgiveness brought freedom I didn't expect. It took effort, and sometimes it was harder than others. But Holy Spirit reminded me—God had forgiven me countless times. Then came the hardest step—forgiving myself. Carrying shame kept me from fully experiencing His love, but letting go freed me. With every act of forgiveness, my heart opened more to Him. How is God calling you to release unforgiveness today?

Seeking love, but finding the Father

I once searched for love in all the wrong places. But as I let go, I saw love wasn't a reward—it was already mine. Father loved me long before I turned to Him. I could never earn His love, only receive it. True love comes from God—we can't love fully without Him. How can you rest in His love and extend it to others today?

37

Walking as the Father sees me

When I saw myself through my Father's eyes, I walked differently. My purpose wasn't clear yet, but He was leading me. He drew me closer, teaching me to trust, love, and follow. I wasn't there yet, but I was learning to embrace the journey. The more I followed, the more He revealed. What step will you take today to walk in the truth of how He sees you?

Mindset Shift: Choosing Faith Over Fear

Trusting God's plan even when unclear

I had been growing spiritually, deepening my relationship with both Father and Holy Spirit, when I was asked to take a temporary role. I said no—twice. Then Holy Spirit said, "You're doing this." I obeyed and walked into dysfunction, judging those around me. But who was I to judge? Hadn't I made mistakes too? Where is pride keeping you from seeing God's purpose?

…

Saying yes: obedience reveals the heart.

I thought I had surrendered—until I stepped into a new job. I felt out of place and wanted to leave, but obedience wasn't just about showing up. Staying forced me to face my own pride, control, and expectations. God wasn't just working through me; He was working in me. Where is God using discomfort to reveal what still needs to be released?

Humility's test: letting go of control

I wanted purpose, but God wanted patience. I thought I was ready to step into something greater, but He saw areas in my heart that still needed refining. Humility meant surrendering my timeline and trusting that waiting wasn't wasted. I had to stop striving and learn that growth happens in stillness, not just motion. Where is God asking you to trust His process instead of forcing your own?

/ 41

Shaping reality: the power of thoughts

During this season, a guest pastor at my church preached a message. I don't remember his name, but the lesson stayed with me. He taught the power of aligning thoughts with God's truth. As I replaced negative thoughts with Scripture and spoke God's promises, my thinking began to change. So did my life. Are your thoughts working for you or against you?

Mind renewal: transforming thoughts every day

God was preparing me for my purpose, but I had to stop striving and let Him lead. Like the car wash lesson, I wanted to take control, but transformation happened when I followed His direction. Not every thought needed action—some needed releasing. As I surrendered, clarity replaced confusion. Where is God asking you to trust His leading instead of figuring it out on your own?

Active trust: standing firm in obedience

God was leading me, but trusting Him required action. When a product recall at my job demanded Sunday shifts, I refused—I wouldn't give up my ministry. It felt risky, but obedience mattered more than approval. I didn't realize how much that decision would shape what happened next. Obedience isn't just personal; it has a ripple effect beyond us. Where is God asking you to trust Him despite uncertainty?

Divine lessons: purpose in every season

I wanted to move forward, but God was teaching me right where I was. I expected purpose to come sooner, but He was using this season to refine me for it. Even in uncomfortable seasons, His hand was at work, shaping me for what was next. The lesson wasn't just patience—it was trust in His process. Where is God asking you to find purpose right where you are?

45

Seeing others through God's loving eyes

A new leader took over at work who clearly cared only about operational success. I struggled with her leadership. Then God asked me to thank Him for bringing her into my life. At first, I resisted. But as I obeyed, my heart softened—and so did she. Over time, my obedience changed everything—workplace dynamics, relationships, even how I saw myself. Where is God asking you to see someone through His eyes?

Trusting God's timing in unfolding purpose

After I obeyed and let go of control, God led me to coaching and even paid for my certification. I thought my purpose would begin immediately, but He had more refining to do. I coached part-time, waiting for Him to release me. It was three years before He said, "Now it's time." Purpose unfolds in His timing, not ours. Where is God asking you to trust His process?

Words create: speak life into being

Still in corporate work and coaching part-time, I waited for God's timing. Instead of complaining, I chose gratitude and began to speak life—declaring truth, hope, and possibility over my circumstances. Proverbs says life and death are in the power of the tongue. Holy Spirit led me to the book, *The Power of I Am* by Joel Osteen, which deepened my understanding. What words are you speaking today?

Stepping into the unknown: trusting God

I didn't know my corporate season was ending—until Holy Spirit said it was time. My coaching business wasn't full, and my husband had been laid off. On paper, leaving made no sense. But I had learned to trust God's timing. I gave my notice without knowing what was next. Faith moves forward, even when the full plan isn't clear. Where is God asking you to take the next step?

Answer the Call; Embrace Your Purpose

Purpose is bigger than your profession.

As I searched for my purpose, I was convinced I had no special gifts or talents. I watched others thrive in their callings and wondered, Was I absent the day God handed them out? But looking back, I was living my purpose every time I listened, encouraged, and showed compassion. What if your purpose has been with you all along?

50

Trials strengthen you for God's purpose.

I once saw hardships as obstacles. Now I see them as training grounds. Every struggle refined my character, deepened my faith, and sharpened my resilience. Purpose isn't just about passion—it's about preparation. God allows trials to equip us for the impact we're meant to make. How has God been preparing you through challenges?

Step forward boldly with God's gifts.

I used to believe my gifts weren't enough. But God doesn't call the ready—He calls the willing. My gifts were there, but they required action. When I stopped waiting for confidence and started using them, clarity followed. God moves when we move. Faith grows in action, not hesitation. Are you using your gifts now, or waiting for a perfect moment that may never come?

Honing your gifts is your responsibility.

Recognizing my gifts was just the beginning—developing them required work. We must refine our talents from God. I had to move from listening to learning to coach, teach, and lead. My first certification wasn't about a title—it was about becoming who I was created to be. Excellence requires effort, and God honors preparation. What steps can you take to develop and use your God-given abilities?

God provides when we obey Him.

God provided funds for my coaching certification, but when He called me to the program, *Train the Trainer* with Jack Canfield, it required a bigger investment. I told God, "If this is my path, You'll have to pay for it." Holy Spirit led me to ask my former employer for the money. It felt bold—too bold. But I obeyed. He wrote the check immediately. Where is God asking you to trust Him for provision?

Faith sustains when the path's unclear.

Leaving my corporate job was a leap of faith, but what came next required greater trust. Doubt crept in—not about God's direction, but about how it would unfold. Faith isn't only one big step—it's a choice to keep walking when the path remains unclear. Trust grows not in certainty, but in the waiting. Where is God asking you to move forward, even when you can't see the outcome?

Purposeful work brings fulfillment and joy.

When I stepped into coaching full-time, something clicked. For the first time, I felt fully alive. That's the power of aligning with God's design. Purpose-driven work isn't just about making a living—it's about making an impact. True fulfillment comes when we walk in what we were created for. Are you pursuing success, or are you pursuing purpose?

56

The Holy Spirit reveals deeper calling.

Jack Canfield's training gave me tools, but Holy Spirit revealed my true purpose. I wasn't only meant to teach Success Principles—I was called to infuse them with deeper spiritual truth. My coaching was always spirit-led, but now God wanted me to integrate the Success Principles with faith. Life isn't just about success—it's about transformation. Are you allowing Holy Spirit to lead you beyond what the world teaches?

Alignment with God unlocks supernatural momentum.

The moment I surrendered fully to my calling, things shifted. Clients, connections, and resources aligned effortlessly—not because I forced them, but because I was in position. When we align with God's will, He orchestrates what we could never arrange ourselves. Are you striving to make things happen, or surrendering to God's perfect alignment?

58

Your calling impacts more than you.

Even when I questioned my value, God never did. Purpose isn't about what we feel—it's about what God has already placed inside us. My journey wasn't just for me—it was for the people I was called to serve. Coaching wasn't about building a business; it was about transforming lives. Who is waiting on the other side of your yes?

Release Doubt and Judgement: Elevate Spirit

Take responsibility and transform your reality.

I believed life was happening to me—until I learned Jack Canfield's first principle: "Take 100 percent responsibility for your life." But Holy Spirit took it deeper. My thoughts, words, and focus weren't just shaping my reality—they were creating it. I could stay the same or take ownership and create something different. Ownership—not blame—was the key to freedom. What reality are you creating with your focus?

60

No one else controls your emotions.

Holy Spirit had already taught me that no one makes me mad, sad, or happy—joy is a choice. Mastering this principle required deep reflection, and I realized that if someone's words hurt, it was their struggle, not mine. But my reaction? That was my choice. Taking ownership of my emotions freed me from blame and resentment. Who are you still giving power over your feelings?

Release blame and reclaim your power.

Blame kept me stuck. As long as I held others responsible for my pain, I gave away my power. Holy Spirit showed me that freedom comes through ownership, not excuses. Jack Canfield's teaching reinforced this—until I took full responsibility, nothing would change. Blame only delayed my healing. Letting go wasn't weakness; it was strength. Who or what do you need to stop blaming?

The words you speak create reality.

Holy Spirit revealed that my words didn't just reflect my thoughts—they created my experiences. I had already learned to shift my mindset, but now I saw an even deeper truth. What I spoke over time became my reality. Complaints fed my struggles, while gratitude unlocked blessings. Speaking life wasn't just positive thinking—it was spiritual responsibility. What reality are you creating with your words?

What you focus on expands greatly.

Holy Spirit told me long ago that when I focus on the problem, I don't see His solution. I've seen this daily—when I focus on possibilities, God's leading, and my next steps, I move forward. But when I dwell on obstacles, they only grow. My thoughts, words, and energy give power to what I focus on. Where is your focus leading you—toward growth or limitation?

Judgment blocks love, healing, and growth.

Judgment creeps in, but Holy Spirit reminds me to pray for people instead of judging them. I once felt irritated by someone constantly promoting themselves and stepping on others' toes. Then Holy Spirit whispered, "This isn't about them; it's about you." That hit deep. Judgment blinds us to our own healing. When I prayed instead, my heart softened. Where is judgment keeping you from love, healing, and growth?

Letting go of unforgiveness brings peace.

God had forgiven me countless times, yet I hadn't always extended that same grace to others. As my awareness grew, I noticed when judgment surfaced and learned to release it to God. Holy Spirit showed me that unforgiveness didn't just affect me—it hindered my relationship with God. Surrendering it brought peace and freedom. Where is unforgiveness keeping you from a deeper connection with Him?

66

Seek God first, let Him lead.

One day, during morning prayer, as I thanked Father for being sovereign, Holy Spirit revealed a truth: seek Him first, and He will direct my steps. Sometimes He resolves the problem, sometimes He leads me to pray, and sometimes He tells me to ask someone else. The point was always to go to Him first. Where are you still looking elsewhere for what only God can provide?

Trust God's plan, not your expectations.

I kept handing situations to God, then taking them back. That didn't feel like trust, but Holy Spirit showed me that releasing control is a process. When I nearly threw out a plant that looked dead, Holy Spirit said, "Keep watering—things aren't as they seem." Weeks later, new growth appeared. Not seeing progress doesn't mean God isn't working. What is God asking you to trust Him with today?

Releasing judgment leads to spiritual elevation.

Holy Spirit continued revealing deeper layers of judgment within me. Each time I thought I had released it fully, another area surfaced. Judgment wasn't just about others—it was about how I saw myself. As long as I held onto it, I was limiting my own growth. Spiritual elevation wasn't about knowing more—it was about loving more. Where is judgment still keeping you from rising higher?

Walk in love, live in freedom.

Releasing judgment wasn't the end—it was the beginning of something greater. Holy Spirit showed me love is the highest elevation. Each day, I choose to walk in trust, joy, and love. Some days are easier, but when I align with God, I feel lighter and free. Living in freedom isn't about perfection—it's about choosing love daily. How will you walk in greater love and freedom today?

Embrace What Is: Find Serenity Within

Accept reality, stop resisting the present.

Fighting reality only led to frustration. Holy Spirit showed me that peace comes when I accept the present moment, trusting that God is working—even when I don't understand. Instead of asking why something is happening, I've learned to ask, "God, how do You want me to grow through this?" Surrendering to what is opens the door to peace. Where are you resisting what is?

71

Shift focus to what you control.

I wasted energy resisting what I couldn't change—replaying the past, worrying about what was next. But acceptance was just the beginning. Holy Spirit showed me that peace comes from surrender, not control. Byron Katie's book, *Loving What Is* reinforced that suffering comes from arguing with reality. I focused on what I could influence and found more peace. Where are you wasting energy on what you can't change?

Clear your messes, incompletes, and tolerations.

I used to overlook small messes, unfinished tasks, and loose ends. But Jack Canfield's core principle, "Clean Up Your Messes and Your Incompletes," showed they matter. Each unresolved issue drained my energy and focus. Holy Spirit showed me that clutter—physical, mental, or emotional—blocks clarity and progress. The more I cleaned up, the lighter I felt. What unfinished business is weighing you down today?

Energy flows where attention consistently goes.

I discovered that where I invest my energy determines my peace. Holy Spirit showed me that focusing on problems only magnifies them, but nurturing gratitude, faith, and purpose expands peace. Whatever we give attention to, we amplify. These shifts transformed my life so much that I now use them in coaching. Where is your energy flowing, and is it creating more peace or more struggle?

Release expectations and trust God's plan.

I thought letting go meant giving up, but Holy Spirit showed me it was really about trust. I kept holding onto my own plans, believing things had to unfold a certain way. But trusting God's plan meant believing His way was always better than mine. When I stopped forcing outcomes and surrendered, doors opened in ways I never expected. Where are expectations keeping you from fully trusting God?

75

Serenity comes from aligning with truth.

I thought peace would come when circumstances changed. But Holy Spirit revealed that true serenity comes from aligning with God's truth—not my emotions, fears, or assumptions. The more I trusted God's truth instead of my own understanding, the more peace I found. Truth isn't always comfortable, but it always sets us free. Where are you seeking peace outside of the truth God has already given you?

Highest and best use of energy

I used to drain my energy on everything—worry, busyness, distractions that didn't serve me. Holy Spirit revealed that peace comes from investing energy wisely—on what truly matters. When I prioritized faith, purpose, and aligned action, I felt lighter and more fulfilled. Your energy is precious—where you invest it shapes your life. Are you using your energy in the highest and best way?

Find gratitude in the present moment.

Gratitude isn't a result—it's a choice. Holy Spirit showed me that peace doesn't come from waiting for circumstances to change, but from recognizing blessings now. The more I focused on abundance instead of lack, the more joy I felt. Nothing steals joy faster than dwelling on what's missing. What if you embraced gratitude right now, trusting that God is already working? What blessings are present in this moment?

Trust God's timing, even when waiting.

Waiting felt like a test—until Holy Spirit reminded me that God isn't just working on my circumstances, He's working on me. I wanted answers now, but He saw what I couldn't. When I let go of my timeline and trusted His, things fell into place in ways I never expected. Delays aren't denials—they're divine appointments in disguise. Where is God asking you to trust His timing today?

Begin and end each day intentionally.

Each day begins with a choice—react to life or prepare for it. Holy Spirit led me to create intentional morning and evening practices, starting with gratitude, affirmations, and prayer, and ending with reflection and release. These simple shifts brought deep peace and helped me embrace what is instead of resisting. We don't drift into alignment—we choose it daily. What small practice will help you cultivate peace?

Recognize Our Teachers—Divine Guidance's Whispers

Every moment holds lessons and opportunities.

Nothing in life is random—every experience carries meaning. Holy Spirit revealed that even the smallest moments hold lessons and opportunities. The grumpy cashier, the delayed flight, the unexpected conversation—each moment invites us to react in frustration or respond with grace. What if every inconvenience was an opportunity for growth? Look around. What lessons and opportunities are waiting for you today?

Teachers appear unexpectedly in your life.

Some of my greatest teachers weren't mentors or coaches—they were unexpected people and experiences. Holy Spirit showed me that wisdom often comes through challenges, strangers, and even setbacks. The hardest moments often teach the most, if we're willing to see the lesson. God places teachers everywhere—sometimes in places we least expect. Who or what is teaching you something right now?

Frustration offers lessons and growth opportunities.

Frustration can feel like a setback, but Holy Spirit showed me it's often an invitation. A last-minute change disrupted my plans, and I questioned why God allowed it—until that delay led to a conversation I wouldn't have had otherwise. What seemed like an obstacle was actually divine alignment. Frustration often masks hidden blessings. Where is frustration inviting you to grow today?

Difficult people refine patience and grace.

I quit praying for patience—every time I did, God sent more chances to practice. Holy Spirit revealed that difficult people weren't obstacles but divine assignments to strengthen grace. My reaction mattered more than their actions. Would I mirror frustration or reflect love? Patience isn't given, it's developed. The more I responded with grace, the less power frustration had over me. Who is teaching you patience today?

Your reactions create learning or resistance.

Every experience offers a choice—learn from it or resist it. Holy Spirit revealed that self-awareness was the key. My reactions weren't just responses; they were shaping my reality. When I resisted lessons, frustration followed. But when I leaned in, wisdom unfolded. Growth isn't about avoiding challenges; it's about responding differently. How are your reactions shaping your journey—are they leading to growth or keeping you stuck?

Be present. Opportunities are happening now.

Life moves fast, making it easy to miss what matters. Holy Spirit keeps reminding me that the greatest lessons and opportunities are right in front of me. But without awareness, I'll overlook them. Every moment holds something valuable, but distractions keep us from seeing it. God is always speaking, but are we listening? What opportunities are unfolding before you right now, waiting for your attention?

A kind word can shift everything.

A simple word can change the energy of a moment. At the grocery store, in traffic, or passing a stranger—kindness has power. A smile, a compliment, or encouragement doesn't just affect others, it shifts something within us. We never know who needs a reminder that they matter, but God does. How can you use your words to bring light to someone's day today?

Discernment unveils Divine lessons and choices.

Not everything is as it seems. That day in the so-called "church," I felt the energy, but it wasn't holy. I didn't recognize it then, but deception was at work. Ever since, I've prayed daily for discernment. Some moments teach, some test, and some require walking away. God reveals truth when we slow down, pray, and listen. What lesson or decision is God revealing to you today?

Pain carries messages and growth potential.

Pain isn't the enemy—it's a messenger. For years, I numbed or pushed it down, but pain kept resurfacing, demanding my attention. Every time I resisted, I stayed stuck. Holy Spirit nudges me to remember that pain isn't here to break me but to awaken me. When I stopped fighting and asked, "What is this teaching me?" healing began, and strength emerged. What is pain revealing to you today?

When you're ready, the lesson appears.

Some lessons can't be rushed. Looking back, I see wisdom hidden in past struggles—I just wasn't ready to receive it. God reveals truth at the right time, never too soon or too late. Every challenge, every person, every moment has prepared me for what's next. You're not just learning—you're becoming. Now, it's time to see beyond where you've been… and step into what's possible.

See It, Believe It, Become It

Let love lead—see what's possible.

Fear keeps us small, convincing us to settle for less than what's possible. But when we look through God's eyes, we see beyond limitations and into divine potential. I used to let doubt dictate my choices, but faith showed me another way. Love expands, while fear restricts. When I chose love, possibilities opened that I never imagined. What might be possible if you led with love instead of fear?

91

Envision it—align with Divine creation.

Holy Spirit had already taught me the power of my words—how they shaped my reality. Jack Canfield and other mentors introduced me to visualization, showing me how to see my goals as already achieved. But God took me deeper. It wasn't just about success—it was about aligning my vision with His. When I did, new possibilities opened. What future are you willing to see before it appears?

Clarity brings focus—what's your desire?

For years, I wasn't sure what I truly wanted. I explored different paths but never felt fully aligned. Then, I asked myself: What desires did God place in my heart?—not what I thought I should want, but what resonated deeply. God's plan became clearer when I stopped second-guessing and started getting intentional. What are you ready to claim with clarity and focus?

See it clearly—step into possibility.

Once I understood the desires God placed in my heart, I had to see them as possible. Visualization wasn't just about imagination—it was about aligning my vision with God's plan. When I started seeing my future through His lens instead of my expectations, I moved with confidence. Clarity fuels belief, and belief fuels action. What possibilities are waiting for you to see them clearly today?

Feel it deeply— activate your vision.

Seeing the vision was just the beginning—I had to feel it as real. My Vision Book had an image of this book before I ever wrote a word. Each time I looked at it, I felt gratitude, excitement, and certainty. Prayer and devotion fueled my faith, and God's plan unfolded. Manifesting His vision starts with thanking Him for what we have. What will you bring to life next?

Keep watering: unseen growth takes faith.

I kept giving situations to God, then pulling them back—over and over again. Trust didn't come instantly. Holy Spirit showed me it's built through practice. I nearly tossed a plant that looked dead, but He whispered, "Keep watering." Weeks later, it bloomed. Faith means showing up when results aren't visible. What blessing might grow if you stay faithful a little longer?

Faith creates—believe before you see.

Faith isn't just hoping for the best—it's trusting that what God placed in my heart is already unfolding. I had to believe in the vision before I saw evidence of it, even when doubt whispered otherwise. When I aligned my faith with His plan, doors opened in ways I never expected. What are you being called to believe in before it becomes visible?

97

Take aligned action—walk in expectation.

Faith without action is just a wish. When I truly believed in what God placed in my heart, I didn't just wait—I moved. Taking aligned action signaled my trust in His plan, even when I couldn't see the whole picture. Faith comes alive when we walk forward in expectation. Where is God calling you to take bold action today?

Trust God's timing—everything unfolds perfectly.

I often questioned why my coaching business wasn't growing as quickly as I expected. But looking back, I see how God was preparing me—shaping my message, refining my skills, and bringing the right people at the right time. If growth had come faster, I wouldn't have been as ready. God's timing is never off, it's always perfect. Where is He asking you to trust the process today?

99

Let go—step into divine flow.

Most of my life, I planned every detail, trying to control how things unfolded. But life became lighter when I trusted God's bigger plan. Instead of forcing outcomes, I leaned into divine flow—expecting goodness, welcoming surprises, and finding joy in the unknown. The best things happened when I let go and let God move. Where can you release control and embrace what's unfolding?

You are ready—step into purpose.

Looking back, I see how every moment—every lesson, delay, and breakthrough led me here. Nothing was wasted. Now, I no longer wonder if I'm ready. I know I am. And so are you. Seek God first, open your heart, and He will direct your steps, bringing the people and opportunities you need. Trust Him, take the first step, and step fully into the life He created for you.

Acknowledgments

Writing this book has been a journey of faith, healing, and obedience, and I could not have done it alone.

First and foremost, all glory to my Heavenly Father, my Lord Jesus, and Holy Spirit. You called me to this work, sustained me through every step, and spoke through me as I wrote each word. Thank You for Your endless grace, love, and patience as I learned to trust Your process.

To my family, thank you for your unwavering love, encouragement, and belief in me—even when I doubted myself. Your presence in my life is a gift I cherish beyond words.

To my friends, mentors, and spiritual leaders, thank you for walking alongside me, lifting me up in prayer, and reminding me of who I am in Christ. Your wisdom and support have strengthened me more than you know.

To Jack Canfield, your Success Principles have played a key role in my personal transformation, equipping me with the tools to take responsibility for my life, shift my mindset, and help others do the same. The phrase "See It, Believe It, Become It," which appears as a chapter title, is one you've often shared, and I include it here with deep appreciation for your impact on my journey.

To DD Watkins, thank you for your *Dream Big* Vision Books and for showing me the power of aligning my vision with faith and action.

To Joel Osteen, your book *The Power of I Am* helped me reframe my self-talk, step into confidence, and declare truth over my life.

To my publisher and editor, thank you for bringing this book to life. Your dedication and expertise have helped turn a vision into reality, and I am beyond grateful for your guidance and partnership.

To Jenni Butz, thank you for giving me the final nudge I needed to say yes to this journey. Your encouragement came at just the right time, and your introduction to Pacelli Publishing opened the door for this dream to become a reality. I'm so grateful our paths crossed.

And to you—the reader—this book was written with you in mind. My prayer is that through these pages, you find hope, healing, and the courage to step into the fullness of who God created you to be. You are seen, you are loved, and you are meant to rise and shine.

With deep gratitude, *Cheri L. Jackson*

About the Six-Word Lessons Series

Legend has it that Ernest Hemingway was challenged to write a story using only six words. He responded with the story, "For sale: baby shoes, never worn." The story tickles the imagination. Why were the shoes never worn? The answers are left up to the reader's imagination.

This style of writing has a number of aliases: postcard fiction, flash fiction, and micro-fiction. Lonnie Pacelli was introduced to this concept in 2009 by a friend, and started thinking about how this extreme brevity could apply to today's communication culture of text messages, tweets and Facebook posts. He wrote the first book, *Six-Word Lessons for Project Managers*, then he and his wife Patty started helping other authors write and publish their own books in the series.

The books all have six-word chapters with six-word lesson titles, each followed by a one-page description. They can be written by entrepreneurs who want to promote their businesses, or anyone with a message to share.

See the entire ***Six-Word Lessons Series*** at **6wordlessons.com**

www.ingramcontent.com/pod-product-compliance
Lightning Source LLC
Chambersburg PA
CBHW070643050426
42451CB00008B/283